Cha Chili

Winning chili recipes of the world's top competitors

How to win a cookoff
By Bill Renfro

The Road to Terlingua
An essay on Chili lore and chicanery
By Kirby Warnock

Table of Contents

A portion of the proceeds from this book's sale goes to Big Bend Education Corp., the driving force behind the national campaign to establish a high school for Big Bend-area students. It raised $600,000. Previously, children had to rise at 4:30 a.m. and travel 160 miles roundtrip each day to Alpine, Texas.

Now the non-profit, 501 (3C) organization is raising funds to build a school/community library at Big Bend High School, then a gymnasium-cafeteria-auditorium. The charity is run by volunteers so nearly all of the donations goes directly to its good works in the Big Bend-Terlingua-Study Butte community.

For further information, or to make a tax-deductible donation, write:

*Big Bend Education Corp.
P.0.256
Terlingua, TX 79852*

How to Win a Cookoff

*Bill Renfro has participated in too many chili competitions to enumerate.
He has an office crammed with trophies to show for the years he's breathed
fire. He has judged all of the major championship cookoffs. And although
he once set himself aflame (actually, he torched the towel tucked into his
belt), this native Texan knows his chili con came. Bill is CEO of family-run,
Fort Worth-based Renfro Foods, which produces award-winning salsas sold
around the country, in Europe and even Mexico. Here, he shares some closely
held secrets about just what makes a good bowl of red:*

Chili competitors have three things in common: They all want to
win. They all want to make good chili. They all realize they're not
going to win every weekend.

It might be months (or years) between wins, but they like the
camaraderie and getting away from the worries of the world or
their workaday lives. And the friendliness is genuine. They'll help
one another. Some of the more established cooks will even provide a
recipe to help newcomers get started. Of course, it might not be ex-
actly their winning formula, but it'll get beginners on the right path.

Many times, if their winning recipe is printed in the newspaper,
or even this book, a crucial ingredient – a particular spice or chili
powder – might be omitted or an amount changed.

Then there are some, like a Chili Appreciation Society International – Terlingua winner named Doris Coats, who will say: "They
can cook my recipe, but they can't cook my chili." She believes that
others won't be able to master the techniques just from reading a
recipe. It takes time and experience.

There are some chili basics. While there are recipes included here that
might contain beef along with chicken and pork, most use only beef, and

it's usually the "mock tender" cut, cubed or coarsely ground. Most winning recipes use onions and fresh peppers like jalapeños and serranos. Some use tomatoes, some don't.

But the spices determine the flavor and make a chili distinctive. Competitors will use different amounts of oregano and comino (cumin). Then there are the chili powder and chili peppers. (I prefer using mainly chili peppers; I'll put a little Gebhardt's chili powder in toward the end.)

Beginners make some obvious mistakes – too much grease and old spices. Old spices lose their flavor; cayenne pepper will lose its heat. Some entries have too much grease. While chili needs some to give it flavor, you don't want to overdo it. Chili swimming in grease is just not attractive. Too much of one ingredient, particularly the spices, marks a losing chili.

A great chili is smooth, not too loaded with any one pepper or spice – just a blended nice taste with an afterburn, perhaps from cayenne or another pepper. This will allow you to taste the chili; then you get some burn at the back of the mouth. It doesn't have to be severe. It needs to be from warm to hot in the back of the throat. And that's what the judges are looking for. You don't want it so hot that you can't taste the chili. A lot of judges look for smoothness in the gravy, so there are not any little particles of what I call "dirt" in it.

Aside from balancing the flavor, the hardest part is getting the meat cooked just right. The perfect chili has meat so tender that you can chew it twice and it disintegrates. It can't be too tender, it can't be mushy, it can't be tough. It's difficult to achieve the right "all dente" texture because of such variables as the weather, the heat, the atmosphere, which can affect how the chili cooks.

As for color, I always strive for a good red. It can be reddish to brown, dark brown.

When I first started to compete, we would cook four hours. Now, contestants typically cook two or two-and-a-half hours. I have always believed that the longer you cook, the smoother the gravy, a better blending of the spices. And that's the difference between competition chili and home chili. At competitions, a major portion of the spice is dumped in during the last 20 minutes before turn-in, to give it full impact.

Veteran competitors are very serious about their cooking but display a relaxed attitude. But most realize that a lot of it is luck and the selection of judges that day. Many factors are involved, and most cooks know that they just can't win every time.

And having built up a reputation as a top competitor won't help. Measures are taken, such as using identical plastic foam cups, ensuring that the judges are unaware of just who is behind each sample. Entries are judged in groups. Should a lot of the best find themselves on a single table and, say, only the top eight from each group advance, some very good ones can get dropped early.

Cookoff chili and home chili are miles apart. With competition chili, you try to concentrate the taste in one spoonful. At home, you want to eat a bowl full. This is not to say competition chili is not good, but after a few bites, you might find it a bit strong. Most judges will have one taste, and it's judged on that one spoonful.

It might come as a surprise to many that, as a Texan and long-time chili cookoff participant, I am not dogmatic on the issue of beans – outside of competitions. Traditionally, beans are a separate dish in Texas and competitions at the start disallowed any legume – kidney or otherwise. It hasn't changed. But at home, I put out bowls of onions, shredded cheese and beans, and let people put in whatever they want.

Bill Renfro, Fort Worth, Texas

All Roads Lead to Terlingua

By Kirby F. Warnock

The transformation of chili from a poor man's meal to a cultural phenomenon is the making of a Texas legend. And you know what they say about truth and legend: "When the truth meets the legend, print the legend."

So I come not to bury chili, but to praise it. Chili has moved from the realm of a basic food group to a sense of self-awareness and celebration. Just like Texas, chili is a state of mind. How this simple bowl of red got to this point is an interesting tale of media, fame and myth-making; most of it rooted in truth.

To set the stage, we must first travel back to the late 1960's. America was straining under a backbreaking load of guilt and angst over the assassinations of John F. Kennedy, Martin Luther King and Bobby Kennedy.

It was the era of the war in Vietnam, bell bottoms, hippies and anti-war protests and the "Summer of Love." Chili, and everything associated with it, was definitely out. Tofu, bean sprouts and brown rice were the choices of the flower children who dominated the popular culture at that time. Everything associated with chili (cowboy hats, boots) was so uncool, so redneck.

Creation of a Craze

In the midst of the swinging 60's, a plan was hatched that would put chili in front of the world, and almost single-handedly make the dish chic again. It all started in Dallas, by a group of men sitting around talking over a pot of chili and cocktails. One evening in 1967, racecar designer Carroll Shelby, David Witts, Bill Neal, Tom Tierney and *Dallas Morning News* columnist Frank X. Tolbert got together for a chili dinner prepared by Wick Fowler. During the evening, Carroll Shelby mentioned some property he owned down in the Big Bend area near an old ghost town named Terlingua. Shelby said that he wanted to sell the property, but couldn't find anyone who knew anything about it. What was needed, he said, was some type of publicity stunt. Tierney mentioned that maybe a chili cookoff should be held.

The idea was pounced on immediately, particularly by Tolbert. As a popular newspaper columnist, he could reach millions of readers, thereby whipping up a media feeding frenzy. He got his chance by appealing to America's oldest rivalry: Texas versus New York. Food writer H. Allen Smith had just published an article in the *New York Times* titled, "Nobody Knows More About Chili Than I Do." It included his recipe for chili that included beans. The argument soon came from Wick Fowler that if you knew beans about chili, you knew chili didn't have beans.

Tolbert went to work, publicizing a cookoff that would settle the issue. It would be held in the ghost town of Terlingua, between H. Allen Smith and Wick Fowler. The winner would be crowned the World Chili Champion.

Hallie Stillwell, the justice of the peace in Brewster County was asked to serve as a judge and Queen of the Chili Cookoff. Other Texas luminaries were tapped into service and the whole thing came together as only something in Texas could. Despite the disorganized efforts of its promoters, it succeeded wildly. Terlingua is about the most remote site you can choose for a world championship of anything. It is not close to any major city and the nearest commercial airport is almost 270 miles away in Midland. Just getting to Terlingua requires a major effort. Despite this inconvenient location, on cookoff day a substantial crowd had made its way out to the middle of the Chihuahuan desert.

The cultural superiority of Texas over New York was at stake when Smith and Fowler turned in their chili entries to the judges. Aware of the PR value of the moment, the judges declared a tie, meaning that everyone had to come back and do it again next year. For some reason, the entire surreal picture of a mass of beer-drinking people crowded around two men stooped over two black pots of chili in the middle of nowhere while a country-western band played was just what people were looking for in 1967. America needed some silliness in the midst of the gloom and melancholy that pervaded the country in the late 60's. For some reason, the Terlingua chili cookoff seemed to fill the bill of comic relief for a weary nation. The cookoffs continued and grew larger. During the first weekend in November, the population of Terlingua swelled from 12 to 1,000.

The topper came in 1974 when Heywood Hale Broun, a contributor to *Sports Illustrated*, took a CBS Evening News camera crew to Terlingua and broadcast the annual craziness to millions of TV viewers. Decades before CNN. MTV or the Internet, most people tuned into the CBS Evening News because of its popular anchorman. Walter Cronkite. On this night, folks sat in their living rooms from New York to San Francisco and watched grown men wearing stuffed armadillos on their heads, eating chili and hollering out loud. It was a wild celebration of chili, in a huge open flat spot in the desert. The World Championship Chili Cookoff had become the Woodstock of the pop media culture. Of course, Tolbert did everything he could to keep the bandwagon rolling. A steady stream of columns in the *Dallas Morning News* extolled the good times in Terlingua. Wick Fowler soon began selling his own Wick Fowler's Three-Alarm Chili Mix at local stores. Chili was not only in the mainstream media, but on your local grocer's shelf. Another shot in the arm came when Jerry Jeff Walker released his best-selling album Viva Terlingua. Despite its title, the record had nothing to do with Terlingua (and was actually recorded in Luckenbach), but the anthems, by Ray Wylie Hubbard and Gary P Nunn's London Homesick Blues, were immediately adopted as the theme songs for the World Championship Chili Cookoff. (To this day, Gary P. Nunn still headlines at the Fowler/Tolbert Cookoff.) Chili now had its own media, songs and product. Things were going good – too good.

The War Starts

The popularity of the World Championship Chili Cookoff meant that everyone wanted to be a cook in Terlingua. To facilitate some kind of selection process, qualifying cookoffs were held around the country under the auspices of the Chili Appreciation Society) International (C.A.S.I.). A. Vann York and Ray King took on the responsibility of running C.A.S.I. and sanctioning the qualifying cookoffs. The logo (designed by Frank X Tolbert II) was a chili pepper with a map of the world emblazoned on it. Cookoffs sprang up; sponsors vied to have their signs at cooksites, and it looked as if there might be a profit to be made.

In 1974, unbeknownst to the rest of the original organizers, Carroll Shelby was granted a trademark for the term "World Championship Chili Cookoff." From now on, he declared, the cookoff would be held just outside Los Angeles, California. (Of course, it wasn't a coincidence that Shelby was now selling his own brand of chili mix.)

The original Terlingua crowd felt that Shelby's actions were underhanded at best, and sneaky at worst, because he filed for his trademark without informing them of his actions. Tolbert was the most upset at what he considered this act of betrayal.

In a fit of anger, he told Shelby to, "Take your damned cookoff to California and save yourself the freight." The Terlingua cookoff was promptly sued by Shelby, who wanted to block its use of the name "World Championship Chili Cookoff."

While this legal fistfight was under way, another split occurred. By now C.A.S.I., headed up by York and King, had become the sanctioning body for chili cookoffs. The days of just showing up at Terlingua with your chili pot and a good line of BS were over.

Nonetheless, Tolbert appeared with two cooks who had flown in from Germany and England and asked that they be entered into the Terlingua cookoff. C.A.S.I. would not allow the foreign cooks to enter because they had failed to qualify. Tolbert argued that there was no C.A.S.I. cookoff in Europe, and his cooks should be allowed to enter anyway. C.A.S.I. stood firm, and the two foreign cooks were turned away.

"That really upset my father," says Tolbert II, the late columnist's son.

Indeed it did. The die was cast. In 1983, the Tolbert-Fowler faction split off from C.A.S.I. and held a competing cookoff on the same day, just a few miles up the road. A lawsuit was filed over who held the rights to the C.A.S.I. name and logo.

There were now three cookoffs, each claiming to be the "true" world championship, although by now both of the Terlingua cookoffs had started referring to themselves as the "International" chili championships because of Carroll Shelby's legal victory to use the term "world" championship.

After a long, bitter trial in front of federal Judge Lucious Bunton, the C.A.S.I. logo and trademark were awarded to York and King. Estimates are that each side spent close to $40,000 a piece in legal fees. The Tolbert/Fowler group had lost, but vowed to continue holding its cookoff, billing it as "The Original Terlingua International Chili Cookoff."

Without a governing body like C.A.S.I., Carroll Shelby set up his own International Chili Society (JCS) to determine the qualifiers for his "world championship," which moved to Las Vegas, Nev.

On the first weekend in November, approximately 5,000 people descend upon a flat, open spot in the desert of Big Bend to hold two chili cookoffs about four miles from each other. The C.A.S.I. cookoff is the larger of the two. but the Tolbert/Fowler cookoff still draws a good crowd. Tolbert, Fowler, Smith and the 27-time Queen of the Chili Cookoff Hallie Stillwell, are all gone now. Tierney is still alive in Dallas, and York lives near the C.A.S.I. cookoff site, operating a restaurant in Study Butte. (By the way, the food there is great.) Today, the Tolbert/Fowler cookoff is run by Frank X's daughter, Kathleen. She, along with a devoted group of volunteers, labors long and hard to keep the memory of her late father alive each year.

However, the bitterness over the legal fight has not completely subsided. Although there was some talk about the two cookoffs coming together, an agreement could not be reached. While some of the blatant animosity between C.A.S.I. and the Tolbert/Fowler groups has toned down a bit (they don't belittle each other in their press releases any more), both groups still harbor a resentment for Carroll Shelby. A popular phrase once heard at Terlingua was, "Don't Cali-fornicate our chili," referring to Shelby's early rival cookoff in Los Angeles. Years ago, Shelby sold his chili mix company to Kraft Foods, and liquidated his Terlingua holdings.

The setting itself is almost surreal; Nestled near the former ghost town of Terlingua, in the heart of the Big Bend, the Chisos Mountains provide a stunning backdrop in the distance against huge, blue sky. If you walk a few yards away from the cookoff areas, you can scare up a covey of blue quail, or see a rattlesnake sunning itself on a rock.

Terlingua itself was once a bustling boomtown, employing 2,000 Mexican miners to extract mercury ore (cinnabar) until the mercury market collapsed after World War I. Chicago financier Charles Perry closed the mine, and the town essentially emptied overnight. Today, there are still miner's shacks littering the hillside, and the town's old cemetery holds its dearly departed in a setting right out of a Sergio Leone Western. When it's chili cookoff time, hundreds of

RVs lumber down the two-lane black-top into town. Every available motel room is rented at nearby Study Butte (pronounced Stoody Bewt) and Lajitas. Tents are pitched on acres of rocky ground, and bizarre, gaudy booths – resembling a cross between a flea market and a Shriners convention are erected. With no hookups or facilities, participants must truck in everything, from water to generators.

On Saturday morning during the cookoffs, what was once no more than a slow spot along Highway 170 is now a colorful sea of humanity. Indeed, most of the fun comes from people watching, not from chili tasting. It must be a fact of life that a slight state of inebriation enhances the taste buds for chili. How else can you explain a booth that hands out free shots of tequila at 9:00 a.m.? The music and pace accelerates throughout the day, culminating in the announcement of the winners, and the ever-popular wet T-shirt contest. You can take your pick of either the C.A.S.I. or the Tolbert/Fowler cookoff, but unabashed silliness and a *joie de vivre* rule both camps.

Like folk music and Las Vegas, a trip to Terlingua is something everyone should do at least once in their lifetime. Plan ahead (it's a long way from anywhere), book your rooms now, and head south to the granddaddy of all chili cookoffs. Viva Terlingua! (Editor's Note: The author would like to state for the record that he likes both cookoffs and is treated well by both camps.)

Reprinted with permission from Big Bend Quarterly

Chili Numero Uno

World's First Chili Championship, 1967
International Chili Society
H. Allen Smith (tied with Wick Fowler)

4 lbs. coarse-ground sirloin or tenderloin
Olive oil or butter
1 or 2 4-oz. cans tomato paste (or fresh tomatoes, finely
chopped or canned tomatoes pressed through
a colander)
3 or 4 medium onions, chopped
1 bell pepper, chopped
2 to 10 cloves garlic, minced
1 tbsp. oregano
1/2 tsp. sweet basil
1 tbsp. cumin seed or ground cumin
Salt and pepper to taste
3 tbsps. chili powder or more, to taste (or some chili pods)

In a 4-quart pot, brown meat in oil or butter, or a blend of the two. Add the remaining ingredients, simmer 2 to 3 hours with the lid on.

Woody's Chili

Second Annual World's Championship, 1968
International Chili Society
Woodruff DeSilva, Ontario, California

5 medium onions, chopped
Small amount cooking oil
Salt and pepper to taste
4 lbs. chuck beef, coarse chili grind or chopped into thumb nail- sized pieces
5 cloves garlic, minced
4 tbsps. oregano
2 tsps. woodruff (an herb)
1 tsp. cayenne pepper

2 tbsps. paprika
Scant tsp. to full tsp. chipeños (also known as chilipiquines), crushed (available at stores stocking Mexican groceries)
4 dashes Tabasco sauce
3 10-oz. cans tomato paste
1 6-oz. can water
4 tbsps. masa harina (Mexican corn flour)

In a skillet, brown onion in oil, seasoning with salt and pepper. Place in chili pot. Brown beef in skillet, adding more oil if necessary. Add garlic and one tablespoon oregano. Add this mixture to the chili pot. In a paper sack, shake together the woodruff, cayenne pepper, paprika, New Mexico chili powder, cumin, the remaining three tablespoons of oregano and the chipeño. Add the blended spices to the chili pot. Further brown beef in chili pot with the Tabasco sauce, tomato sauce and tomato paste. Add enough water to cover the meat and simmer at least two hours. Cool the chili, then refrigerate overnight. Skim off the excess grease. Reheat the chili to the boiling point and stir in a paste made of the masa flour and a little water to thicken the mixture. Stir constantly to prevent sticking and scorching, adding water as necessary for the desired texture.

C.V. Wood's World's Championship Chili

Third and Fifth Annual World's Championship, 1969 & 1971
International Society
C.V. Wood, Beverly Hills, California

3 lbs. stewing chicken, cut into pieces
1-1/2 quarts water or 6 14.5-oz. cans chicken broth
1/2 lb.beef suet or 1/2 cup vegetable oil
4 lbs. flank steak
5 lbs. thin, center-cut pork chops
6 long green chilies, peeled
2 tsps. sugar
3 tsps. ground oregano
3 tsps. ground cumin
1/2 tsp. monosodium glutamate (MSG), optional
3 tsps. pepper
4 tsps. salt
5 tbsps. Gebhardt's chili powder
1 tsp. cilantro (coriander)
1 tsp. thyme
8 oz. Budweiser beer
4 15-oz. cans tomato sauce
1 cup celery, finely chopped
2 cloves garlic, finely chopped
3 medium onions, diced
2 green peppers, cut into 318 inch pieces
1 lb. Jack cheese, grated
1 lime
Dash of Tabasco sauce

Combine chicken with water in a large pot and simmer 2 hours. Strain off broth and reserve chicken for other use, or use canned chicken broth. Render suet to make 6 to 8 tablespoons of oil or use cooking oil. Trim all fat and bones from pork and cut it into quarter-inch cubes. Trim all fat from flank steak and cut it into 3/8-inch cubes.

Boil chilies 15 minutes or until tender. Remove seeds and cut the chilies into 1-inch squares. Mix sugar, oregano, cumin, MSG, pepper, salt, chili powder, cilantro and thyme with beer until all lumps are dissolved. Add the tomatoes, celery, chilies, beer mixture and garlic to the chicken broth.

Pour about a third of the reserved suet or oil into a skillet, add pork and brown. Do only half total amount at a time. Add the pork to the broth mixture. Cook slowly 30 minutes.

Brown beef in the remaining oil, about one-third of the total amount at a time. Add the beef to the pork mixture and cook slowly about one hour. Add onions and peppers. Simmer 2 to 3 hours until meat is broken down, stirring with a wooden spoon every fifteen to 20 minutes.

Cool one hour and refrigerate 24 hours. Reheat chili before serving it. About 5 minutes before eating, add grated cheese. Just before serving, add the juice of the lime and stir the mixture with a wooden spoon. Makes six servings.

2-Alarm Chili

Fourth Annual World's Championship, 1970
International Chili Society
Wick Fowler, Austin, Texas

2 lbs. meat, coarsely ground or diced
8-oz. can tomato sauce
2 cups water
1 package of 2 Alarm Chili ingredients*
Salt

Sear the meat until it becomes gray. Add tomato sauce and water. Add all the ingredients except the masa flour in the chili packet. Cover kettle and simmer one hour and 15 minutes, until meat is tender. Stir occasionally. Skim off excess grease.

Mix masa flour with warm water into a smooth paste. Stir into chili to tighten it and add flavor. Simmer 15 to 20 minutes and salt to taste. Chili is ready to serve. Serves six.

For 1-Alarm, use half of the red pepper in the chili packet. For False-Alarm Chili, leave out the red pepper. For 3-Alarm Chili or hotter, add hot pepper.

*2-Alarm Chili mix is available in many areas. Developed by Wick Fowler, its ingredients have been kept a proprietary secret of the Caliente Chili Company of Austin.

Chili Man Chili

Seventh & Ninth Annual World's Championship, 1973 & 1975
International Chili Society
Joe DeFrates, Springfield, Illinois

1 lb. ground beef
1 1-oz. envelope Chili Man Chili Mix*
1 8-oz. can tomato sauce
1 dash Tabasco sauce

Brown ground beef in heavy skillet. Stir in contentss of chili mix and add tomato sauce. Simmer for one hour and add Tabasco. Serves four.

*Chili Man Mix was created by Defrates, who began marketing it in the 1950s, later selling the recipe to the Milnot Co. of Litchfield, Ill. The blend is available in the Midwest. Actual ingredients are a proprietary secret.

Chili Rockies Style

Sixth Annual World's Championship, 1972
International Chili Society
Howard Winsor, Colorado

1 medium onion, chopped in blender
5 or 6 large cloves garlic, chopped in blender
1 cup water
2 lbs. lean beef, cut into 1/4-inch cubes
1 lb. pork, cut into 1/4-inch cubes
7 oz. can Ortega brand green chilies, including liquid
5 or 6 jalapeño peppers
1 14-oz. can whole tomatoes, chopped in blender
1 16-oz. can whole tomatoes, chopped in blender
4 large bay leaves
1 tbsp. oregano
1 tbsp. salt
1 tsp. cumin powder

Chop onion, garlic and water in blender. Cook until soft. Add meat; cook until it loses red color. Add green chilies and jalapeño peppers to the blender and puree to make a chile pulp. Add one cup chile pulp and tomatoes to meat; cook 20 minutes with pot covered. Add other seasonings.

Remove bay leaves about halfway through cooking time. (You might have to remove lid last part of cooking time if chili is too thin). Total cooking time is approximately three hours. If you want to use beans, put in bottom of bowl before adding chili. Serves six to eight.

Allegani Jani's Chili

Eighth Annual World's Championship, 1974
International Chili Society
Jani Schofield-McCullough, Midland, Texas

4 lbs. stew meat, ground once
3 onions, chopped
2 tbsps. oil
Salt and pepper to taste
2 heaping tsps. cumin seeds
6 cloves garlic, mashed
1 8-oz. can tomatoes
1 tsp. sugar
1 12-oz. can beer
2 packs chili powder
3 tsps. mole paste (available in stores stocking Mexican groceries)
1 tsp. Tabasco sauce
1 tsp. salt
1 quart water
4 jalapeño peppers, chopped
1 cup masa harina (Mexican corn flour, available in stores stocking Mexican groceries)

Brown meat and onions in oil. Season with salt and pepper. Using a molcajete (a Mexican grinding tool), grind cumin seeds and garlic with a little water. Add to meat. In a blender, combine tomatoes, sugar, beer, chili seasoning and chili powder. Add to stew along with mole paste, Tabasco sauce, salt, water and jalapeño peppers. Cook two hours, stirring well from time to time.

After two hours, make a runny paste of masa and water, adding it to the stew to thicken it. Stir the stew rapidly while adding the paste to keep it from getting lumpy. Cook another hour.

Chili, Valdez Style

10th Annual World's Championship, 1976
International Chili Society
Rudy Valdez, New Mexico

1 lb. pork shoulder, chopped into 3/8 inch pieces
1 lb. beef flank steak, chopped very finely but not ground
1 tsp. cumin, divided into two portions
1 ripe tomato, chopped
1 clove garlic, minced
1 medium white onion chopped
6 6-inch long stalks celery, chopped
1 8-oz. can Ortega green chile salsa
I 8-oz. can Ortega green chile peppers, diced
1 tsp. oregano
1 tsp. Tabasco sauce
1 tbsp. hot New Mexico chili powder
1 tbsp. medium New Mexico chili powder
I heaping tbsp. mild New Mexico chili powder
Water
Salt to taste

Cook pork and beef in separate pans for 20 minutes. Add 1/2 teaspoon cumin to each skillet. In a 6-quart saucepan, combine tomato, garlic, onion, celery, chile salsa, green chilies, oregano and Tabasco sauce. Make a paste, adding a small amount of water, with the three grades of chili powder and add it to the vegetable mixture in the saucepan. Cook mixture 20 minutes. Drain the juice from the meat, except four tablespoons. Add the meat to the vegetable mixture. Cook about one hour or until the meat is tender. Just prior to serving, add salt to taste.

Jay's Chili

11th Annual World's Championship, 1977
International Chili Society
Jay Pennington, Washington, D.C.

1 tbsp. cooking oil
3 medium onions, finely chopped
2 bell peppers, finely chopped
2 celery stalks, finely chopped
3 garlic cloves, finely chopped
8 lbs. coarse ground round steak
2 No. 2 cans tomato sauce
2 No. 2 cans stewed tomatoes
2 No. 2 cans water
1 6-oz. can tomato paste
1 4-oz. can chile salsa
1 3-inch green canned hot pepper,finely chopped (only 1 chile)
2 3-oz. bottles Gebhardt's chile powder
1 4-oz. can green diced chilies
Dash of oregano
Salt to taste (approximately 3 tbsps.)
Pepper (course ground) to taste
Garlic salt to taste

Put oil in a 10-12 quart pot. Add onion, bell pepper, celery and garlic cloves. Cook until onion is transparent.

Add meat gradually, stirring until the redness disappears. Add remaining ingredients, stirring after each addition.

Lower heat and simmer two to three hours. Stir frequently to prevent scorching. Serves 12-16.

Nevada Annie's Champion Chili

12th Annual World's Championship, 1978
International Chili Society
LaVerne Harris, Las Vegas, Nevada

3 medium onions
2 medium green peppers
2 large stalks celery
2 small cloves garlic
1/2 (or more) small fresh jalapeños
8 lbs. lean chuck, coarsely ground
1 7-oz. can diced green chilies
2 14-oz. cans stewed tomatoes
1 15-oz. can tomato sauce
1 6-oz. can tomato paste
2 3-oz. bottles Gebhardt's chili powder
2 tbsps. cumin
Tabasco sauce to taste
1 12-oz. can Budweiser beer, divided into two portions
1 12-oz. bottle mineral water
2 or 3 bay leaves
Garlic salt to taste
Salt and pepper to taste

Dice and saute the first 5 ingredients. Add the meat and brown. Add remaining ingredients, including 1/2 can beer, then drink the remainder as needed.

Add water to cover top of chili mixture. Cook about three hours on low heat, stirring often. Makes 24 or more servings.

Reno Red

13th Annual World's Championship, 1979
International Chili Society
Joe & Shirley Stewart, San Francisco, California

3 lbs. round steak, coarsely ground

3 lbs. chuck steak, coarsely ground

1 cup vegetable oil or suet

1 3-oz bottle of Gebhardt's chili powder

6 tbsps. cumin

2 tbsps. monosodium glutamate (MSG)

6 small cloves garlic, minced

2 medium onions, chopped

6 dried chili pods, remove stems and seeds and boil 30 minutes in water (1 3-oz bottle New Mexico chili pepper)

1 tbsp. oregano, soaked in cup of beer

2 tbsps. paprika

2 tbsps. cider vinegar

3 cups beef broth

1 4-oz. can diced Ortega green chilies

Half a 14-oz can stewed tomatoes (or to taste)

Dash of Tabasco sauce

Brown meat in oil or suet, adding black pepper to taste. Drain meat and add chili powder, cumin, MSG, garlic and chopped onions. Cook 30 to 45 minutes using as little liquid as possible. Add water only as necessary. Stir often.

Remove skins from boiled pods, mash pulp and add to meat mixture (or add New Mexico chili powder), oregano and beer mixture, paprika, vinegar, two cups of beef broth, Ortega green chiles, stewed tomatoes and Tabasco. Simmer 30 to 45 minutes. Stir often. Dissolve masa flour in remaining beef broth, pour into chili mixture. Simmer 30 minutes, stirring often.

Capital Punishment Chili

14th Annual World's Championship, 1980
International Chili Society
Bill Pfeiffer, Washington, D.C.

1 tbsp. oregano
2 tbsps. paprika
2 tbsps. monosodium glutamate (MSG)
9 tbsps. chili powder (light)
4 tbsps. cumin
4 tbsps. instant beef bouillon, crushed
2 12-oz. cans beer
2 cups water
4 lbs. extra lean chuck, chili ground
2 lbs. extra lean pork, chili ground
1 lb. extra lean chuck, cubed
2 large onions, finely chopped
10 cloves garlic, finely chopped
Half cup vegetable oil or suet
1 tsp. powdered mole
1 tbsp. sugar
1 tsp. coriander
1 tsp. Tabasco
1 8-oz. can tomato sauce
1 tbsp. masa harina (Mexican corn flour)
Salt to taste

In a large pot combine paprika, oregano, MSG, chili powder, cumin, beef bouillon, beer and two cups water. Let simmer.

In a separate skillet, brown meat with one tablespoon of oil or suet until meat is light brown. Drain and add to simmering spices. Continue until all meat has been added.

Saute finely chopped onions and garlic in one tablespoon of oil or kidney suet. Add to spices and meat mixture. Add water as needed. Simmer two hours. Add mole, sugar, coriander, Tabasco and tomato sauce. Simmer 45 minutes.

Dissolve masa in enough warm water to form a paste. Add to chili. Add salt to taste. Simmer 30 minutes. Add additional Tabasco to taste.

"Chili, from the Texan pronunciation of chile (Spanish for the pepper of the Capsicum family; originally from the Nahuatl word chilil, *is a thoroughly Texan food found on menus throughout the state. It's possible the word entered the Texan vocabulary before the Spanish linguistic corruption of chili to chile was complete, in which case Texans can correctly refer to hot peppers as 'chilis' (much to the dismay of New Mexican pepper snobs)."*

– Joe Cummings, *Texas Handbook*

15th Annual World's Championship, 1981

International Chili Society
Fred Drexel, Van Nuys, California

1 lbs. beef brisket, cut into 1-inch cubes
1 lb. lean ground pork, cubed
1large onion, chopped fine
2 tbsps. vegetable oil
Salt and pepper to taste
2 to 3 cloves of garlic, minced
2 tbsps. diced green chilies
1 8-oz can tomato sauce
1 beef bouillon cube
1 12-oz. can Budweiser beer
1 cup water
4 to 6 tbsps. Gebhardt's chili powder
2 tbsps. ground cumin
1/8 tsp. dry mustard
1/8 tsp. brown sugar
Pinch of oregano
Dash of Tabasco

In a large iron kettle or Dutch oven, brown beef, pork and onion in heated oil. Add salt and pepper to taste. Add remaining ingredients. Stir well. Cover and simmer three to four hours, until meat is tender and chili is thick and bubbly. Stir occasionally. Makes four to six servings.

Los Venganza del Alamo Chili

16th Annual World's Championship, 1982
International Chili Society
Bill Pfeiffer, Texas

1 tbsp. oregano
2 tbsps. paprika
2 tbsps. monosodium glutamate (MSG)
11 tbsps. Gebhardt's chili powder
4 tbsps. cumin
4 tbsps. instant beef bouillon, crushed
3 12-oz. cans beer
2 lbs. thick butterfly pork chops, cubed
2 lbs. chuck, cubed
6 lbs. ground rump roast
4 large onions, finely chopped
10 cloves garlic, finely chopped
1/2 cup vegetable oil or suet
1 tsp. powdered mole (mole poblano)
1 tbsp. sugar
2 tsps. coriander seeds
1 tsp. Tabasco sauce
1 8-oz. can tomato sauce
1 tbsp. masa harina (cornflour)
Salt to taste

In a large pot, combine paprika, oregano, MSG, Gebhardt's chili powder, cumin, beef bouillon, beer and two cups of water. Let simmer.

In a separate skillet, brown meat one pound at a time with tablespoon of oil or suet for each batch until all meat is light brown. Drain and add to simmering spices. Continue until all meat has been added.

Saute finely chopped onions and garlic in one tablespoon of oil or suet. Add spices and meat mixture. Add water as needed. Simmer two hours. Add mole, sugar, coriander, and tomato sauce. Simmer 45 minutes.

Dissolve masa flour in enough water to form a paste. Add to chili. Add salt to taste. Simmer 30 minutes. Add Tabasco to taste.

"Chili – a bowl of blessedness."

– Will Rogers

Taos Timber Chili

17th Annual World's Championship, 1983
International Chili Society
Harold R. Timber, Taos, New Mexico

1 tbsp. sugar
8 oz. beef consomme
2 tsps. oregano
2 tbsps. paprika
2 tbsps. cumin
1 tbsp. celery salt
7 tbsps. Gebhardt's chili powder
2 tbsps. monosodium glutamate (MSG)
1 tsp. cayenne pepper
1 tsp. garlic powder
1 tsp. mole
2 cups warm water
Vegetable oil, enough to saute meat
2 lbs. beef chuck, cut into 3/8-inch cubes
2 lbs top round, coarsely ground
2 lbs. pork butt, medium ground
3 cups finely minced onion
2 tbsps. garlic, finely minced 1 cup green chilies, chopped
20 oz. of tomato sauce
1 12-oz. beer
1 tbsp. masa harina (Mexican cornflour) (optional)

Combine first 10 ingredients and dissolve in warm water. Place mixture in a 6-quart pot, bring to a boil, then simmer.

In a frying pan, saute meat in a small amount of oil. Add to main pot.

Saute onion and garlic, then add to pot with green chilies. Add tomato sauce. Bring pot to boil. Add beer. Simmer uncovered for 1-1/2 to 2 hours, stirring occasionally. Let stand for 1/2 hour. Skim off excess grease. Correct seasoning to taste.

To thicken, mix masa with enough water to make a paste. Blend thoroughly with chili mixture.

Cover and let stand one hour before serving.

In 1972, chili was declared the State Dish of Texas through a legislative bill proposed by Rep. Ron Bird of San Antonio and Rep. Ben Grant of Marshall.

Bottom of the Barrel Gang Ram Tough Chili

18th Annual World's Championship, 1984
International Society
Dusty Hudspeth, Irving, Texas

2 lbs. beef, chili grind
1 8-oz. can tomato sauce
1 onion, finely chopped
1 tsp. garlic powder
1/4 cup Gebhardt's Chili powder
1 tsp. oregano
1 tsp. salt
2 tsps. ground cumin
1/4 tsp. Tabasco sauce
1/2 tsp. cayenne pepper
1/2 12-oz. can beer
1 tbsp. vegetable oil

Sear meat in covered 2-quart pot with vegetable oil. Add tomato sauce, onion and garlic powder, cover. Simmer 30 minutes, stirring occasionally.

Add remaining ingredients. Stir, simmer for one hour. Add water if necessary.

Serve with side dishes of pinto beans, chopped onions and grated cheddar cheese as garnishes. Serves six to eight.

Shotgun Willie Chili

19th Annual World's Championship, 1985
International Chili Society
Carol and Dave Hancock

6 New Mexico dried chile peppers
6 dried pasilla peppers
I tbsp. oregano leaves
6 lbs. prime beef, cubed or coarse ground
4 medium onions, finely diced
1 15-oz can tomato sauce
4 cups beef broth
2 tbsps. vinegar
I tsp. Tabasco sauce

1 6 tbsps. Gebhardt's chili powder
2 tbsps. ground cumin
1 tsp. cayenne pepper
1 tbsp. MSG
1/2 tsp. sugar
14 garlic cloves, minced
1 cup water
2-3 tbsps. vegetable oil
Black pepper & salt to taste

Remove stems and seeds from pepper pods and boil chile peppers in water for approximately one hour until pulp separates from skin. Scrape pulp from skin, mash into a paste. Use one cup of this paste in recipe. Boil oregano leaves in one cup of water. Steep like tea and strain, retaining the liquid.

Brown beef, a small batch at a time in hot oil, adding onions and black pepper to each batch. Remove meat to chili pot after it browns. Add remaining ingredients, including the oregano water. Blend well. Cover and simmer two hours, stirring occasionally.

Sespe Creek Chili

20th Annual World's Championship, 1986
International Chili Society
Jim Beaty, California

2 lbs. beef sirloin, cut into 3/8-inch cubes
2 tbsps. vegetable oil
5 cloves garlic, crushed into paste
1 tsp. seasoned salt
1/2 8-oz. can tomato sauce
1/2 10-oz. can beef broth
1 10-oz can chicken broth
8 tbsps. Gebhardt's chili powder
1 tsp. oregano

2 tsps. cumin
2 tsps. hot New Mexico chili powder (use milder grade if less heat is desired)
2 onions, chopped
1/2 cup chopped yellow onions
1/2 tsp. mole (optional)
1/8 tsp. coriander powder
1/2 tsp. monosodium glutamate (MSG)
1 tsp. Tabasco sauce

Brown meat, 1 pound at a time, in oil. Drain and put in chili pot with chopped onions, beef broth, chicken broth, chili powder, oregano, cumin and chopped onions.

Mix well and simmer for two hours.

Add crushed garlic, seasoned salt, tomato sauce, chili powder, mole, coriander and MSG. Cook 20 minutes then add Tabasco sauce. Use beef broth to thin. Salt to taste. Serves six to eight.

Margo's Chili

21st Annual World's Championship, 1987
International Chili Society
Margo Knudson, Loomis, California

1 tbsp. oregano leaves
5 to 7 cloves garlic, crushed
2 medium onions, chopped fine
2 oz. Gebhardt's chili powder
3 lbs. tri-tip cut beef, cubed or
  coarsely ground
3 oz. sausage
2 tbsps. kidney suet or vegeta-
  ble oil
1/2 oz. salt
1/2 oz. chile pepper powder
1/2 tsp. Hot New Mexico chili
  powder

1/2 oz. cumin
White pepper to taste
1/2 tsp. coriander (optional)
4 to 6 oz. tomato sauce
1/2 pint beef broth, add water
  if necessary
1 medium Ortega pepper,
  minced
1/2 tsp. cayenne pepper
Dash of Tabasco sauce

Place oregano leaves in very hot water; let steep. Put aside.

Saute onions and garlic in suet or oil about three minutes. Add Gebhardt's chili powder and ordinary chile pepper powder, mix well.

Brown beef in separate pan, one pound at a time. Pepper while browning. Add sauteed onion mixture. Add a little broth to keep from sticking. Saute sausage and Ortega pepper together for about two minutes. Add to pot and cook fifteen minutes.

Add remaining spices, tomato sauce, water or broth, and mix well. Cook about 30 minutes.

Add oregano tea. Cook about two hours or until meat is tender, stirring occasionally. During last 20 to 30 minutes, add salt and cayenne pepper if needed. Serves six to eight.

"No one knows for sure when it was created, but mid-1800 accounts of Texas street life seldom fail to mention the 'chili queens' of San Antonio, women who sold bowls of chili from impromptu street stands. The dish seems to have been conceived by Texas cowboys in the 1840s, when they began pounding chilipequins (small, round, very hot chilies; called chiltepines or chiles pequines in today's Mexico), ground spices, and tough, stringy beef into compressed bricks. The bricks were later boiled in pots along the trail to make a stew; the peppers and spices helped preserve the meat and also masked the taste when it began to go bad."

– Joe Cummings, *Texas Handbook*

7/8's Chili

22nd Annual World's Championship, 1988
International Chili Society
Kenton and Linda Stafford, Fillmore, California

3 lbs. beef top sirloin, cut into 1/4-inch cubes
1 tsp. vegetable oil
1/8 tsp. seasoning salt
3/4 tsp. garlic salt
1/4 tsp. garlic powder
1/4 tsp. meat tenderizer
2 13- oz. cans chicken broth
6 oz. beef broth
8 oz. tomato sauce
1/2 medium yellow onion, finely chopped
1/2 medium white onion, finely chopped
3-5 cloves of garlic, finely chopped
5 tbsps. Gebhardt's chili powder
6 tbsps. California chili powder
1 tbsp. and 1 tsp. New Mexico chili powder
1 tbsp. pasilla chili powder
2 tbsps. cumin, finely ground
1 tsp. salt
1/4 tsp. coriander (optional)
1 tsp. Tabasco sauce (optional)
1/2 tsp. oregano
1/4 tsp. cayenne pepper

Brown meat, one pound at a time, with one teaspoon oil, seasoning salt, garlic salt, garlic powder and meat tenderizer. Drain all excess grease. Put meat into cooking pot.

Add one can chicken broth, beef broth, tomato sauce, onions, garlic, Gebhardt's chili powder, 5 tablespoons California chili powder, one tablespoon New Mexico and pasilla chili powders, 1 tablespoon of cumin, 1/2 teaspoon of salt, and optional coriander and Tabasco. Mix well and simmer for 1-1/2 hours.

Add the other can of chicken broth, if needed. Add 1/2 teaspoon oregano, 1/4 teaspoon cayenne pepper, one teaspoon New Mexico chili powder, one tablespoon California chili powder, 1/2 teaspoon salt, one tablespoon cumin and teaspoon garlic salt. Cook another 1 to 1-1/2 hours, stirring occasionally. Salt to taste. Serves six to eight.

> *"If there is any doubt about what the generality of Mexicans think about chili, the* Diccionario de Mejicanismos, *published in 1959, defines chili con carne as 'detestable food passing itself off as Mexican, sold in the U.S. from Texas to New York.'"*
>
> – H. Allen Smith

Pedernales River Rat Chili

1988 Terlingua International Chili Championship CASI
Lynn Hejtmancik, Austin, Texas

2 lbs. chili grind beef chuck roast
1 tbsp. bacon grease

Bag No. 1

3 tbsps. chili powder
1 tsp. garlic powder
2 tsps. onion powder
1/2 tsp. black pepper
1/2 tsp. salt
1/2 tsp. cayenne pepper

Bag No.2

3 tbsps. chili powder
1 tbsp. cumin
2 tsp. garlic powder
1/4 tsp. white pepper
1/2 tsp. oregano powder
Pinch basil
1/2 tsp. MSG (optional)

Other Ingredients

1 14.5-oz. can chicken broth
1 14.5-oz. can beef broth
1 8-oz. can salt-free tomato sauce 1 beef bouillon cube
1/2 tsp. light brown sugar

Heat bacon grease in cooking pot until very hot and smoking. Add room-temperature meat. Cook until brown and making its own juice. Stirring continuously, add broth, and half of Bag No. 1. Cook covered at a medium boil for 45 minutes. Uncover and stir every 10 minutes. Add water as needed. After 45 minutes, add the rest of Bag No.1. Add tomato sauce and Bag No. 2. Add beef bouillon. Add brown sugar.

Use the following to season to taste: Salt, cayenne pepper (for hot "front" taste), white pepper, brown sugar. Ready to eat. Better the next day.

Although there are many theories on the origins of chili, Tomlinson's Book of Texas Records *declared that Tejanos in San Antonio invented the dish, which was first described in print in 1828 by Cincinnati writer J.C. Cooper.*

Yahoo Chili

1989 Terlingua International Chili Championship CASI
Barbara Britton, Mesquite, Texas

Step one ingredients
2-1/2 lbs. beef chuck/mock
    tender or round steak cut in
    1/4-inch cubes
1 tsp. shortening
1 8-oz. can salt-free tomato sauce
1 14.5-oz. can beef broth
2-1/4 cups water
2 tbsps. Texas-style chili powder
1 tbsp. onion powder
1/2 tsp. ground red pepper
2 tsps. beef flavored base or
    instant bouillon
1 tsp. chicken flavored base or
    instant bouillon
1/2 tsp. salt
1 tbsp. chili powder

Step two ingredients
1 tbsp. ground cumin
2 tsps. garlic powder
3 tbsps. Texas style chili powder
1/4 tsp. ground black pepper

Step three ingredients
1/2 tsp. salt
1/8 tsp. ground red pepper
1 tbsp. chili powder
1 tsp. ground cumin
1/2 tsp. onion powder

Step one: In a 5-quart Dutch oven, brown beef in shortening. Do not drain. Add tomato sauce, beef broth, water. Combine seasonings and add to beef mixture. Bring to a boil; reduce heat. Simmer 1-3/4 hours. Add additional water if chili gets too thick.

Step two: Combine second batch of spices. Add to chili. Cover and simmer 30 minutes.

Step three: Combine third batch of spices. Add to chili. Cover and simmer 15 minutes. Makes six servings.

Tarantula Jack's Thundering Herd Buffalo Tail Chili

23rd Annual World's Championship, 1989
International Chili Society
Phil Walter, Seattle, Washington

3 lbs. beef, cubed
2 medium Walla Walla sweet
  onions, chopped finely
3 large cloves garlic, finely
  minced

2 10-oz cans of chicken broth
2 12-oz cans tomato sauce
7 tbsps. Gebhardt's chili
  powder
2 tbsps. ground cumin
1/4 tsp. Tabasco sauce

Saute beef in skillet. Transfer beef to your favorite chili pot and simmer with onions, garlic and broth for 1-1/2 hours. Keep covered. Add the tomato sauce, chili powder and cumin. Cook at least one hour, stirring occasionally.

15 minutes before eatin' time, take off lid and enjoy the aroma of the greatest chili ever. Add Tabasco. Cover and simmer for another 15 minutes. Add salt to taste.

It's now ready to serve. Give out the Pepto Bismol samples to all small children and women who wish to eat yonr chili. Give yonr empty chili pot to the chili groupies and suggest they use new Dawn Detergent to clean it up. (It's the Official Grease Cutter of the International Chili Society.) Comb yonr hair, straighten yonr hat and practice being modest before you receive applause or the championship trophy if you are competing in a sanctioned JCS Cookolf. Serve with a cold Budweiser. This will serve six to eight hungry varmints.
– Phil Walter

High Octane Chili

1990 Terlingua International Chili Championship CASI
Jerry Hunt, Shreveport, La.

Step one ingredients

3 lbs. beef, chili grind
1 10.5-oz can beef broth
1 8-oz. can tomato sauce
4 tbsps. onion flakes
2 tsps. beef-flavored soup base
   or instant bouillon
1 tsp. chicken-flavored soup
   base or instant bouillon
1 tsp. garlic powder
2 tbsps. chili powder
2 tsps. hot pepper sauce

Step two ingredients

1/2 tsp. black pepper
1/2 tsp. onion powder
1/2 tsp. garlic powder
1/2 tsp. white pepper
1 tbsp. ground cumin
1 tbsp. paprika
4 tbsps. chili powder
1/2 tsp. red pepper

Step three ingredients

3 tbsps. chili powder
1 tsp. ground cumin
1/2 tsp. red pepper

Step one: In a Dutch oven, brown beef but do not drain juice. Add beef broth and tomato sauce. Combine remaining ingredients and add to meat mixture. Bring to a boil, reduce heat, cover and simmer 1 hour.

Step two: Combine spices and add to chili. Simmer 45 minutes to 1 hour.

Step three: Combine spices and add to chili. Simmer 30 minutes and serve. Makes eight servings.

Backdoor Chili

24th Annual World's Championship, 1990
International Chili Society
David Valega, Bethany, Oklahoma

Step one ingredients

3 lbs. chuck tender
1-2 tbsps. vegetable oil
2 14-oz. cans of beef broth
1 8-oz can of tomato sauce
4 dashes of Tabasco sauce
1 tbsp. onion powder
3/4 tsp. cayenne pepper
2 tsps. beef bouillon granules

1 tsp. chicken bouillon granules

Step two ingredients

3/4 tsp. garlic powder
1 tbsp. ground cumin
3/4 tsp. white pepper
6 tbsps. Gebhardt's chili
  powder
Salt to taste

Brown meat in oil in chili pot. Add beef broth. Add tomato sauce, Tabasco and remainder of Step one ingredients. Bring to boil and cook until meat is tender. Add water as needed.

30 minutes before serving (being judged), add step two ingredients. Simmer to achieve World's Championship Chili.

Grab a couple of chilled cans or bottles of Budweiser, and get ready to hear the praises. Try to appear modest. — David Valega

Out-O-Site Chili

1991 Terlingua International Chili Championship CASI
Doris Coats, Irving, Texas

Step one ingredients

2-1/2 lbs. beef, chili grind or cubed small
1 tsp. shortening
1 14.5-oz can beef broth
1 8-oz. can tomato sauce
2 tsps. onion powder
2 tsps. garlic powder
1 tsp. beef flavored soup base or instant bouillon
1 tsp. chicken-flavored soup base or instant bouillon
1 cup water

Step two ingredients

2 tsps. ground cumin
1/4 tsp. white pepper
1/2 tsp. ground red pepper
1/2 tsp. salt
1/2 tsp. McCormick "Season All" seasoned salt
1/2 tsp. onion powder
2 tbsps. McCormick Mexican hot chili powder
2 tbsps. McCormick Texas-style chili powder

Step three ingredients

1/4 tsp. ground red pepper
1/4 tsp. salt
2 tsps. paprika
1 tsp. ground cumin
1 tbsp. chili powder

Step one: In a Dutch oven, brown beef. Do not drain juice. Add beef broth and tomato sauce. Combine remaining ingredients and add to beef mixture. Bring to a boil; reduce heat, cover and simmer 1 hour.

Step two: Combine second batch of spices and add to chili. Cover and simmer 45 minutes. Add water if the chili gets too thick.

Step three: Combine third batch of spices and add to chili. Cover and simmer 30 minutes. Makes six servings.

"Chili cookoff beginners make some obvious mistakes – too much grease and old spices. Old spices lose their flavor; cayenne pepper will lose its heat. Some entries have too much grease. While chili needs some to give it flavor, you don't want to overdo it. Chili swimming in grease is just not attractive. Too much of one ingredient, particularly the spices, marks a losing chili."

– Bill Renfro, veteran chili cookoff competitor and judge

Road Meat Chili

25th Annual World's Championship, 1991
International Chili Society
Randy Robinson, Columbus, Ohio

Step 1 ingredients
3 lbs. beef, cubed or chili grind
8 oz. ground pork
1 tbsp. flour
1 tbsp. vegetable oil
1/3 cup onions, diced
1/2 tbsp. granulated garlic
1 14-oz. can beef broth
2 14-oz-cans chicken broth
8 oz. can tomato sauce
1/2 tbsp. ground cumin
1 4-oz. can mild green chilies
1 jalapeño pepper

1 tsp. black pepper
3 tbsps. Gebhardt's chili powder

Step 2 ingredients
1 4-oz. can tomato sauce
4 tbsps. Gebhardt's chili powder
2 tbsps. mild New Mexico chili powder
2 tbsps. ground cumin
1 tsp. granulated garlic
1 tsp. Tabasco sauce
1/2 tbsp. brown sugar

Saute beef in oil, drain. Put meat in a 4-quart cooking pot. Add remainder of Step one ingredients. Simmer one hour, covered. Add all Step two ingredients. Simmer 45 minutes.

Doc's Secret Remedy

26th Annual World's Championship, 1992
International Chili Society
Ed "Doc" Pierczynski, Carson City, Nevada

3 lbs. beef sirloin, London broil
or tri-tip, cubed
4 tbsps. vegetable oil
6 oz. sausage meat or diced
sausage
1 14-oz. can beef broth
1 8-oz. can tomato sauce
1 6-oz. can Snap-E-Tom

12 oz. Budweiser beer
11 tbsps. Gebhardt's chili
powder
1 tsp. garlic powder
1 tbsp. onion powder
2 tsps. Tabasco sauce
1 tbsp. ground cumin
Salt to taste

Saute beef in oil. Fry sausage meat till done; drain well. Put beef, sausage and half can of broth in your favorite chili pot and bring to slow simmer.

Add tomato sauce, half of the beer (drink the rest), six tablespoons of chili powder, garlic powder, onion powder and one teaspoon of Tabasco.

Simmer slowly for about 1-1/2 hours or until meat is tender. Add remainder of chili powder and Tabasco, cumin. Simmer for 30 minutes. Salt to taste. Will feed six to eight hungry interns.

This prescription is good for what ails ya! It is known to cure lumbago, mange, dry rot, blind staggers and a bad hang over. As a precaution for those stomach burners, keep a bottle of Gaviscon handy.

– Ed "Doc" Pierczynski

Cin-Chili Chili

1992 & 1993 Terlingua International Chili Championship CASI
Cindy Reed, Houston, Texas

Step one ingredients

2 lbs. beef chuck tender, cut into 3/8-inch cubes
1 tsp. cooking oil
1 tbsp. dark chili powder
2 tsps. granulated garlic

Step two ingredients

1 8-oz. can tomato sauce
1 14-1/2 oz. can beef broth
1 tsp. chicken bouillon granules
1 tsp. jalapeño powder
1 tbsp. onion powder
2 tsps. garlic powder
1/2 tsp. red pepper
1 tsp. white pepper

16 oz. spring water
1 tbsp. dark chili powder
2 serrano peppers
1/2 tsp. salt

Step three ingredients

1 tbsp. paprika
1 pkg. Sazon Goya
1 tsp. onion powder
1 tsp. garlic powder
1/2 tsp. white pepper
5 tbsps. medium and dark chili powders

Step four ingredients

2 tsps. cumin
1/8 tsp. salt

Step one: In a three-quart heavy saucepan, add first batch of ingredients while browning the meat.

Step two: Combine second batch of seasonings and add to beef mixture. Bring to a boil. Reduce heat and simmer for 1-1/2 hours. Float two serrano peppers.

Step three: Combine third batch of seasonings and add to beef mixture. Bring to a boil. Reduce heat and simmer for 20 minutes. You may add water or beef broth for consistency. Remove serrano peppers when they become soft.

Step four: Add remaining ingredients and simmer for 10 minutes.

Reed made history by winning two consecutive championship titles, in 1992 and 1993.

> *"A great chili is smooth, not too loaded with any one pepper or spice – just a blended nice taste with an aflerburn, perhaps from cayenne or another pepper... And that's what the judges are looking for. You don't want it so hot that you can't taste the chili."*
> – Bill Renfro, veteran chili cookoff competitor and judge

Puppy's Breath Chili

27th Annual World's Championship, 1993
International Chili Society
Cathy Wilkey, Seattle, Washington

3 lbs. beef sirloin or tri-tip, cubed or coarsely ground
2 tsps. vegetable oil
1 small yellow onion, finely diced
1 4-oz. can beef broth
3-1/2 tbsps. ground cumin
1/2 tsp. oregano
6 garlic cloves, finely chopped
3 tbsps. Gebhardt's chili powder
1 tbsp. mild New Mexico chili powder
5-6 tbsps. California chili powder
1 8-oz. can tomato sauce
1 dried New Mexico chile pepper; boiled and pureed
1 14-oz. can chicken broth
1 tsp. Tabasco sauce
1 tsp. brown sugar
Juice of 1 lime
Dash of monosodium glutamate (MSG)
Salt to taste

Brown meat in oil for about hour over medium heat. Add onion and enough beef broth to cover meat. Bring to a boil and cook for 15 minutes.

Add one tablespoon of cumin and teaspoon of oregano. Reduce heat to light boil and add half of the garlic. Add half of the chili powder and cook for 10 minutes. Add tomato sauce with the pulp from the dried peppers and remaining garlic. Add any remaining beef broth and chicken broth for desired consistency.

Cook for one hour on medium heat, stirring occasionally. Add remaining chili powders and cumin. Simmer for 25 minutes on low to medium heat, stirring occasionally. Turn up heat to light boil and add Tabasco, salt to taste, brown sugar and juice of lime.

Simmer on medium heat until you are ready to serve or enter a cookoff.

Keep your Pot Hot!
— Cathy Wilkey

Aside from balancing the flavor, the hardest part is getting the meat cooked just right. The perfect chili has meat so tender that you can chew it twice and it disintegrates. It can't be too tender, it can't be mushy, it can't be tough. It's difficult to achieve the right al dente texture because of such variables as the weather, the heat, the atmosphere, which can affect how the chili cooks.

— Bill Renfro,
veteran chili cookoff competitor and judge

Mountain Express Chili

28th Annual World's Championship, 1994
International Chili Society
Bill and Karen Ray, Riverside, California

4 tbsps. Gebhardt's chili powder
4 tbsps. California chili powder
3 tbsps. mild New Mexico chili powder
3 tbsps. ground cumin
2 tbsps. hot New Mexico chili powder
2 tbsps. flour
1 tbsp. pasilla chile powder
1 tbsp. garlic powder
1 tsp. ground Mexican oregano
1 can (14-1/2 ounces) whole tomatoes
1 can (14-1/2 ounces) chicken broth
4 cups water
2 medium onions, finely chopped
1 garlic clove, pressed
4 lbs. tri-tip or bottom sirloin, trimmed and cut in 1/4-inch cubes
Salt to taste
Tabasco sauce

Combine all dry ingredients in a small container. Remove seeds from tomatoes, then sieve or finely chop. Combine tomatoes, broth, water and dry ingredients in a bowl. Mix well. Put into a chili pot and simmer.

In a skillet, saute onions and garlic in a little water over low heat for 30 minutes. Drain and add to tomato sauce. Simmer 30 minutes. In a large skillet, cook meat until no longer pink. Drain juices and add meat to chili pot.

Simmer for 1-1/2 hours or until meat is tender. Adjust seasoning with salt and add Tabasco if hotter chili is desired.

The Chili Prayer

Lord God, You know us old cowhands is forgetful. Sometimes I can't even recollect what happened yestiddy. We is forgetful. We just know daylight and dark, summer, fall, winter, and spring. But I sure hope we don't ever forget to thank You before we is about to eat a mess of good chili.

We don't know why, in Your wisdom, You been so doggone good to us. The Chinese don't have no chili, ever. Frenchmens is left out. The Rooshians don't know no more about chili than a dog does about a side saddle. Even the Meskins don't get a good whiff of it unless they stay around here.

Chili eaters is some of Your chosen people. We don't know why You so doggone good to us. But lord, God, don't ever think we ain't grateful for this chili we about to eat. Amen.

Attributed to Bones Hooks. a black cowboy cook at a ranch reunion, in *A Bowl of Red* by Frank X. Tolbert, 1972

Doc J's Chili

1994 Terlingua International Chili Championship CASI
Jim Hedrick, Roanoke, Virginia

Step one ingredients

3 lbs. beef chuck, coarse ground beef or cubed
Oil or vegetable shortening
1 can beef broth
1 can chicken broth
1 8-oz. can tomato sauce
1 tbsp. granulated onion
2 tsps. beef bouillon
3 tbsps. chili powder
1 tsp. chicken bouillon
1/4 tsp. red pepper
1 tsp. jalapeño powder

Step two ingredients

1/4 tsp. black pepper
1/2 tsp. onion powder
2 tsps. granulated garlic
1/4 tsp. white pepper
1 tbsp. ground cumin
1/4 tsp. red pepper
3 tbsps. chili powder

Step three ingredients

2 tbsps. chili powder
1 tsp. ground cumin
1/4 tsp. red pepper
1/4 tsp. salt
1/2 tsp. monosodium glutamate (MSG)

This recipe takes three hours to cook. Brown meat in small amount of oil or vegetable shortening. Add tomato sauce and enough broth to cover meat. Bring to a boil. Reduce heat to a simmer and add remaining first batch ingredients. Simmer until meat reaches the proper consistency. Turn off fire and keep covered for 45 minutes. Then turn on heat again and bring mixture to a simmer. 30 minutes before serving, blend in second batch ingredients. Stir well. 15 minutes before eating, blend in remaining ingredients. Stir well. Serve hot.

"Cookoff chili and home chili are miles apart. With competition chili, you try to concentrate the taste in one spoonful. And at home. you want to eat a bowl full."

– Bill Renfro,
veteran chili cookoff competitor and judge

Sierra Chili

1995 Terlingua International Chili Championship CASI
Colleen Wallace, Dallas, Texas

2-1/2 lbs. beef chuck mock tender, cubed or chili grind
1/2 tsp. vegetable shortening
Seasoned salt
1 14.5-oz. can beef broth
1 8-oz can tomato sauce
Water
1 tbsp. Terlingua Won Chili Powder
1 tbsp. granulated onion
1 tsp. granulated garlic
1/2 tsp. cayenne pepper

1/4 tsp. ground jalapeño pepper
1 tsp. beef bouillon granules
1 tsp. chicken bouillon granules
1/2 tsp. salt
4 tsps. ground cumin
1 tsp. granulated garlic
1/4 tsp. black pepper
1 package Sazon Gora
6 tbsps. Colleen Wallace Chili Powder (Available from Pendery's)
1/4 tsp. brown sugar

Brown meat in shortening and seasoned salt. Add broth, tomato sauce and enough water to cover meat plus 1 inch. Add water as needed. Simmer for 30 minutes. Add Terlingua Won chili powder granulated onion, one teaspoon granulated garlic, cayenne pepper, ground jalapeño pepper, bouillon granules and salt. Slow bubble for about one hour or until meat is tender. Add cumin, remainder of garlic, black pepper, Sazon Goya, Colleen Wallace Chili Powder and brown sugar. Simmer for 45 minutes.

A-H Reamer Chili Company

29th Annual World's Championship, 1995
International Chili Society
Norm and Bobbi Gaul, Costa Mesa, California

2 10-1/2-oz. cans chicken
  broth
1/2 8-oz can tomato sauce
3 tbsps. California chili powder
1 tbsp. pure New Mexico chili
  powder
3 tbsps. Gebhardt's chili
  powder
2 tbsps. ground cumin

1 tsp. salt
3 tsps. vegetable oil
1 small onion, chopped
5-7 cloves garlic, minced
2-1/2 lbs. beef tri-tip or bottom sirloin, cut into 1/4-in.
  cubes or coarsely ground
1/2-1 tsp. Tobasco sauce

In chili pot, mix 1-1/2 cans chicken broth and tomato sauce. Stir in chili powders, cumin and salt. Bring to boil.

In a skillet, add one teaspoon oil and saute onions and garlic over low heat until
tender. Add to sauce.

Using same skillet, adding a little oil as needed, saute meat, 1/3 at a time,
until no longer pink and add to sauce. Bring to low boil and let simmer 2-1/2
hours, adding more chicken broth as needed.

One half-hour before serving, adjust seasoning and heat with salt and Tabasco.
Serves six to eight.

Arkansan Chili

1996 Terlingua International Chili Championship CASI
Bo Prewitt, North Little Rock, Arkansas

First step ingredients

2-1/2 lbs. chuck, top sirloin roast or ground chuck, 1/2-inch
 cubed
1 14.5-oz can beef broth
1/4 tsp. monosodium glutamate (MSG)
1 tbsp. granulated onion
2 tsps. granulated garlic
2 tsps. beef bouillon granules
2 tsps. chicken bouillon granules
1/4 to 1/2 tsp. cayenne pepper
1/4 tsp. white pepper
1 tbsp. paprika
1 28-oz. can salt-free tomato sauce

Step two ingredients

2 tbsps. Fort Worth light chili powder
1 tbsp. Gebhardt's chili powder
1 pkg. Sazon Goya
1/2 tsp. brown sugar
1 tsp. ketchup

Step three ingredients

1 pkg. Sazon Goya
1 tbsp. Fort Worth light chili powder
2 tbsps. Gebhardt's chili powder

1/2 tsp. monosodium glutamate
1-1/2 tsps. ground cumin Step four ingredients:
1/4 tsp. red pepper
2 tsps. Fort Worth light chili powder
2 tsps. Gebhardt's chili powder
1-1/2 tsps. ground cumin
1 tsp. garlic granules
1 tsp. onion granules
1/2 tsp. beef soup base granules
1/2 tsp. chicken soup base granules

This is a three-hour recipe. Brown and cook meat for 30 minutes. Add beef broth and Step One spices. Cook 1 hour. Add tomato sauce. Simmer 45 minutes.
Add Step Two spices. Cook 15 minutes. Add water as needed, but don't let it get too thin.
Add Step Three spices. Cook 15 minutes.
Add Step Four spices. Cook 15 minutes.

Southern Chili Georgia Style

30th Annual World's Championship, 1996
International Chili Society
Georgia Weller, Bloomfield Hills, Michigan

3 lbs. chuck, cubed
1 can beef broth
1 can chicken broth
1 8-oz. can tomato sauce
1 4-oz. can green chilies, chopped
3 tsps. vegetable oil
4-1/2 tbsps. California chili powder
4 tbsps. Gebhardt's chili powder
1/2 tbsp. hot New Mexico chili powder
1/2 tbsp. Chimayo chile powder
1/2 tbsp. pasilla chile powder
3-1/2 tbsps. ground cumin
1 tbsp. granulated garlic
4 tsps. onion powder
1/2 tbsp. brown sugar
1 tsp. Tabasco

Brown meat and add to chili pot along with chicken and beef broth, tomato sauce and green chiles.

Add 2/3 of the spices. Cook for two hours.

Add remaining spices. Cook additional hour or until meat is tender. Add salt to taste.

North Texas Chili

1997 Terlingua International Chili Championship CASI
Glenn Dickey, Arlington, Texas

Step One ingredients

2-1/2 lbs. beef mock tender, cubed
1 14.5-oz. can beef broth
1 8-oz. can tomato sauce
1 tbsp. beef bouillon granules
1 tsp. chicken bouillon granules
1 tsp. cayenne pepper
1 tbsp. granulated onion
2 tbsps. paprika
1 tbsp. Fort Worth light chili powder
1/2 tsp. jalapeño powder
1/2 tsp. salt

Step two ingredients

2 tbsps. Gebhardt's chili powder
2 tbsps. Fort Worth light chili powder
2 tbsps. R.T. chili powder
1/2 tsp. white pepper
1 tbsp. ground cumin
1 tbsp. powdered garlic

Brown meat and drain juices. Simmer meat in broth and tomato sauce for 40 minutes.

Add remainder of Step one ingredients. Cook until meat is tender.

Add Step two ingredients. Cook 30 minutes.

Gold Miner's Chili

31st Annual World's Championship, 1997
International Chili Society
Stephen Falkowski, Hopewell Junction, New York

1 tbsp. vegetable oil
3 lbs. beef, cut into 1/4-in. cubes
1-1/2 cups white onions, finely minced
8 garlic cloves, finely minced
3/4 tsp. garlic powder
2 15.5-oz. cans chicken broth, with fat removed
4 oz. tomato sauce
3 tbsps. ground cumin
5 tbsps. mild California chili powder
4-1/2 tbsps. medium New Mexico chili powder
1 tbsp. hot New Mexico chili Powder
2 tsps. salt
1/2 tsp. meat tenderizer
1/2 tsp. light brown sugar
1 tsp. Tabasco sauce

In a large pot, simmer onion and minced garlic in two cups of chicken broth for 10 minutes.

Add tomato sauce and all dry spices, except the tenderizer and sugar. Mix well.

In a separate skillet, brown the meat in oil using a separate pan. Drain well. Sprinkle meat with tenderizer. Add meat to the onion/spice mixture.

Add remaining broth and simmer 2-1/2 hours. Mix in sugar and Tabasco just before serving.

Carol's Own Chili

1998 Terlingua International Chili Championship CASI
Carol West, Wylie, Texas

Step one ingredients
1-1/2 lbs. mock tender, cubed
1 14.5-oz can beef broth
1 8-oz. can tomato sauce
1/2 tbsp. paprika
1/2 tsp. cayenne pepper
1/2 tbsp. onion, powder or granules
2 chicken bouillon cubes
2 beef bouillon cubes
1 tbsp. Carol West chili powder *(Available from Pendery's)*

Step two ingredients
2 tsp. ground cumin
1 pkg. Sazon Goya
1/8 tsp. brown sugar
1 tsp. garlic, powder or granules
1/8 tsp. white pepper
3 tbsps. Carol West chili powder

Brown meat. And broth and tomato sauce. Mix well. Add remaining Step one ingredients. Cook 30 minutes.

Add Step two ingredients. Cook 30 minutes.

24 Karat Chili

32nd Annual World's Championship, 1998
International Chili Society
Kathy LeGear, Dallas, Texas

2-1/2 lbs. beef roast, cubed
2 14-oz. cans beef broth
2 cups water
2 8-oz. cans tomato sauce
2 tsps. vegetable oil

Step 1 spices

1 tsp. monosodium glutamate (MSG)
2 tbsps. onion powder
2 tsps. beef bouillon granules
1 tsp. chicken bouillon granules
1/4 tsp. seasoned salt
1 tbsp. paprika
1 tbsp. Texas chili powder
1 tbsp. ground chilies

Step 2 spices

1 tsp. monosodium glutamate (MSG)
2 tsps. ground cumin
1 tsp. garlic powder
1/4 tsp. seasoned salt
1 tbsp. Texas chili powder
1 tbsp. Gebhardt's chili powder

Step 3 spices
1-1/2 tsps. cumin
1 tsp. onion powder
1 tbsp. Texas chili powder
1/2 tsp. garlic powder
1 tbsp. Gebhardt's chili powder
1 tbsp. Texas chili powder

Step 4 spices
1-1/2 tsps. ground cumin
1 tbsp. Texas chili powder
1/2 tsp. garlic powder

Brown beef in oil. Add beef broth, water, one can tomato sauce and Step One spices. Bring to boil, cover and cook at medium boil until beef is almost tender, about 2-1/2 hours.

30 minutes before eating, add Step Two spices and remaining can of tomato sauce. Simmer.

20 minutes before eating, add Step Three spices. Simmer.

After 10 minutes, add remaining batch of spices. Salt to taste. For added heat, add Tabasco sauce.

Out-O-Site Chili, Too

1999 Terlingua International Chili Championship CASI
Bob Coats, Irving, Texas

Step one ingredients
2-1/2 lbs. beef chuck tender, cubed
1 tbsp. shortening
1 14.5-oz. can beef broth
1 14.5-oz. can chicken broth
1 8-oz. can tomato sauce
2 serrano peppers

Step two ingredients
2 tsps. granulated onion
1/2 tsp. cayenne pepper
2 tsps. Wyler's beef granules
1/4 tsp. salt
2 tsps. Wyler's chicken granules
1 tbsp. Pendery's Fort Worth light chili powder
2 tbsps. Gunpowder Foods Texas red chili powder

Step three ingredients
2 tsps. Pendery's ground cumin
2 tsps. granulated garlic
1/4 tsp. Gunpowder Foods' Hot Stuff
2 tbsps. Gebhardt's chili powder
1 tbsp. Pendery's Fort Worth light chili powder
1 pkg. Sazon Goya

Step four ingredients
1 tbsp. Gebhardt's chili powder
1 tsp. Pendery's ground cumin
1/4 tsp. granulated garlic
1/4 tsp. cayenne pepper
1/4 tsp. brown sugar

Saute beef chuck in shortening until gray. Float serrano peppers and blend in rest of Step one ingredients while keeping half of the chicken broth in reserve.

Add Step two ingredients. Cover and cook 1 hour. Squeeze peppers and discard pulp.

Add Step three ingredients, adjust liquid with remainder of chicken broth, if necessary. Cover and cook 30 minutes.

Add Step four ingredients. Reduce heat to a slow boil and cook 10 minutes. Adjust salt, cayenne, and Gebhardt's chili powder to taste.

"We're the major leagues. They're (Tolbert/Fowler cook-off entrants in Terlingua) the bush leagues. It's unfortunate they didn't qualify to the big show."

— Bob Coats, 1999 CASI champion, as quoted by the *San Antonio Express-News*

Zanjero Red Chili

33th Annual World's Championship, 1999
International Chili Society
Maud Swick, Bakersfield, California

3 lbs. beef roast, coarsely ground or cubed
1 tsp. vegetable oil
1 cup onion, finely diced
5 garlic cloves, crushed
2 Ortega chilies
1 14-oz. can chicken broth
1 14-oz. can beef broth
1 8-oz. can tomato sauce
10 tbsps. chili powder
1/2 tbsp. cumin
1 tbsp. hot New Mexico chili powder

Saute meat and onions in one teaspoon oil. Add chicken broth. Simmer 1 hour.

Add remaining ingredients. Simmer 1 hour. Add salt to taste.

High Country Chili Verde

1999 World Championship Chili Verde
International Chili Society
Joe Barrett

Vegetables

2 lbs. mild green chilies, diced
1 bunch chopped cilantro (fresh coriander)
1 lb. hot green chilies, diced
1 pasilla pepper, seeded and diced
1-1/2 lbs. green tomatillos, husked and quartered
2 jalapeño peppers, seeded, deveined and diced
2 jalapeño peppers, diced
1 bell pepper, seeded and chopped
4 serrano peppers, seeded and minced
2 bunches green onions, chopped
19 oz. Las Palmas green enchilada sauce
2 tbsps. green chili powder
7 tbsps. ground cumin
2 tbsps. monosodium glutamate (MSG)

Meats

3 lbs. pork sirloin tip, cubed
8 cloves garlic, crushed
6 tbsps. lard
1-1/2 lb. sausage, fried and chopped fine
5 oz. canned white chicken meat, drained and chopped
Salt
Tabasco habanero hot sauce

Place all vegetables and powdered spices in large pot and stir well.

Fry pork with garlic in lard until light crust forms on cubes. Drain. Pat dry with paper towels to remove excess lard. Add to pot with vegetables.

Bring to boil. Simmer for one hour, stirring occasionally.

Add sausage. Simmer one hour, stirring occasionally. Add chicken. Simmer one hour, stirring occasionally. Salt to taste.

During last 10 minutes, check for heat and add Tabasco as needed.

Texas-born Bessie Coleman, the world's first licensed black pilot, operated a small but profitable chili parlor in Chicago before going abroad to learn to fly.

Bess' Best Chili

2000 Terlingua International Chili Championship CASI
Dixie Johnson, Lamar, Missouri

3 lbs. beef chuck tender, cubed or chili grind
1 tbsp. shortening
1 8-oz. can tomato sauce
1 can 14.5-oz can chicken broth
1/2 tsp. cayenne pepper
2 tsps. Wyler's instant chicken bouillon
4 tbsps. Pendery's Fort Worth light chili powder
2 serrano peppers, seeded
1 14.5-oz. can beef broth
1-1/2 tbsps. onion powder
2 tsps. Wyler's instant beef bouillon
2 tsps. Pendery's ground cumin
3/4 tsp. Pendery's white pepper
1 pkg. Sazon Goya
1/4 tsp. salt
3 tbsps. Gunpowder Foods Texas red chili powder
1 tsp. garlic powder
1/4 tsp. brown sugar
1/4 tsp. Gunpowder Foods hot stuff
1 tsp. Pendety's ground cumin

Saute beef in shortening until gray. Add tomato sauce, beef broth, 1/2 can chicken broth, beef and chicken bouillon, 1 tablespoon Pendery's chili powder, cayenne pepper, serrano pepper, 1 tablespoon cumin and onion powder. Bring to a boil. Cook for about 1 hour, until meat is tender.

Remove peppers. Add white pepper, Sazon Goya, salt, Gunpowder Foods Texas Red Chili Powder, garlic, cumin, and two tablespoons of Pendery's chili powder. Adjust liquid with remainder of chicken broth or water. Cover and cook 30 minutes.

Add sugar, one tablespoon of Pendery's chili powder, Gunpowder Foods Hot Stuff and cumin. Reduce heat and simmer 10 to 15 minutes. Adjust seasonings with salt and chili powder for "front" and "back" heat.

Dixie Johnson and husband Junior live in Lamar, a town of 5,500 in southwestern Missouri. In 1994, she retired after 36 years with the U.S. Agriculture Stabilization & Conservation Service. After watching Junior cook for two years, Dixie wanted to get involved. She joined CASI in 1986. A year later, she became a co-founder of Mo/Kan Chili Pod. She is the winner of several state titles but also, she says, has left many cook-offs in 14 years "with nothing," advising: "Never give up on your chili."

Jerry Simmon's Chili Verde

World's Championship Chili Verde Cookoff, 2000
International Chili Society
Jerry Simmon, Florissant, Missouri

2 lbs. lean pork, cubed 3/8 to 1/2 inch
2 tbsps. pork suet
1 cup chopped onions
1 can chicken broth

First spice mix

1-1/2 tsps. granulated garlic
2 tbsps. Kraft chicken base
1 tsp. oregano
2 tsps. cornstarch
1 tsp. cumin

Second spice mix

6 oz. hot green chilies
2 tbsps. powdered green chilies
10-minutes-to-go spice mix
13 oz. green chilies, 3/8-in. pieces
1/4 tsp. powdered green jalapeño
8 oz. Herdez salsa verde
8 oz. green Mexican sauce
1 tsp. cumin
1/4 cup cilantro (fresh coriander)

Brown pork in suet. Add onions and broth to the pot. Simmer for one hour. Add first spice mix. Cook until meat is tender. Add water as needed to keep meat covered.

30 minutes before eating, add second spice mix.

With 10 minutes to go, add last spice mix.

Adjust chili for "heat," salt and consistency. Make sure its thick enough.

Must be HOT! Also salty.

> *"The chief ingredients of all chili are fiery envy, scalding jealousy, scorching contempt, and sizzling scorn."*
>
> – H. Allen Smith

Macktown Chili

International Chili Society
34th World Championship Chili Cookoff, 2000
Jim Weller, Bloomfield, Michigan

3 lbs. tri-tip beef, cubed
1 14-oz. can beef broth
1 14-oz. can chicken broth
1 8-oz. can tomato sauce
1 tsp. Tabasco pepper sauce
Water

Spice mix

8 tbsps. mild California chili powder
2 tbsps. hot California chili powder
3 tbsps. ground cumin
1 tbsp. garlic granules
1 tbsp. onion granules
1/2 tbsp. arrowroot

Brown meat, drain and add to chili pot with broths and tomato sauce. Add three-fourths of spice mix. Bring to boil. Simmer 2 hours.

Add Tabasco and remaining spices. Thin with water if necessary. Cook additional half hour or until meat is tender. Add salt to taste. This recipe makes approximately 3 quarts.